Denim Dudes

Contents

Japan and Australia

Introduction

I could start by telling you many amazing facts about denim and jeans: the fact that at any one time, approximately 50 per cent of the global population is wearing a pair of jeans; or that at least 3.9 billion jeans are produced globally per year; or that the world jeans market is worth roughly $75 billion. That got your attention...?

But it's better to talk from the heart and I can truly say that denim is the most important fabric of the twenty-first century, not just for me, but for the majority of the world.

My first realization that I was falling for denim was in 2004 when I visited a famed denim mill in North Carolina, USA. It was there that I realized learning about denim is an endless journey; however much you learn, you never get to the end of the road: the history, the chemistry, the passion. It's both humbling and very very addictive.

I am lucky enough to travel to many corners of the globe to learn, share and hunt for denim. All along the way I meet passionate, exceptional and obsessive characters and this is what inspired me to put this book together: to celebrate all those characters. I also wanted to achieve a balance between the experienced and the new-starters – those who work in denim, those who simply love it and those who wear it every day.

Denim has literally changed, fuelled and made the lives of so many people in this book, including mine. When talking to these obsessives they light up as if talking about a loved one: the eyes sparkle, gestures become animated and you have their attention, heart and soul.

I knew that putting together this book would be a challenge, especially alongside a demanding day job and a schedule filled with events, travel and plenty of jetlag! Most of the work was done on the road: on planes, in hotels and waiting at departure lounges. But the real struggle I discovered was not what to put in, it was what (or more specifically, who) I had to leave out, as it's impossible to feature everyone in just one book. There are geographical gaps in the coverage of this book: Hong Kong, Bangkok, Copenhagen, Osaka … I could only just scratch the surface.

Lastly, there's another notable omission: the ladies! The denim industry is a boys club, there's no doubt about it, but over the years I have had the privilege of meeting some exceptionally knowledgeable and gifted women working in denim, but that's a whole other book.

America

America is the daddy of denim and its denim history revolves around labour, durability and a 'built to last' attitude seen in the original founding brands, such as Levi's, Wrangler, Lee – as well as smaller brands such as Boss of the Road, Headlight and Montgomery Ward. San Francisco remains an epicentre of jeanswear. Brands such as Telleson, Jack Knife and stores such as Self Edge add modern-day kudos. Close by, however, LA has emerged as the modern manufacturing home to all that is indigo. Thousands of denim manufacturers, design houses, global headquarters, laundries, mills and specialist stores stretch from the Stronghold in Venice, through Vernon, home to giant brands such as 7 For All Mankind and Lucky Brand, right up to Eagle Rock's Rising Sun fanatics. On the East Coast New York has its own vibe, and two juxtaposing attitudes of both purist and fashionista. There's the Double RL crew and the PRPS guys pushing the boundaries of vintage and then the '90s kings of the runway, Calvin Klein and DKNY. Add to that the inspirational mix of fashion-week darlings such as Rachel Comey and Phillip Lim and you have a whole lot of something for everyone.

DONWAN HARRELL

Founder of PRPS, New York

Shot in New Jersey

'The jean jacket is an original vintage Levi's Type 1 jacket from the late 1940s. I love the hand-threading repair, mix of panelled denim, the patina on the hardware and the natural colour of the worn denim. It's the best. The military jacket is a vintage 1960s Vietnam permeable A-2 cold weather field jacket. It belonged to a friend of mine who wore it in the war.

'The jean was a limited-edition collaboration with one of the blogs I frequent: Selvedge Yard. Only 50 were made. We thought it would be cool to come up with a giveaway jean to celebrate the coming together of both companies, but it turned into a three-way official effort with Triumph Motorcycles. We printed the bike on the inside pocket bags, and the gas-tank icon as the stitch on the back pocket. It's my personal favourite rope-dyed, Japanese selvedge jean.'

GREG CHAPMAN

Creative director of H. W. Carter & Sons

Shot in Brooklyn, New York

'I've been breaking in selvedge raw denim for over 20 years – ever since I came across a pair of 1950s deadstock Levi's from a vintage store in San Francisco back in '91. I had owned a few pairs of vintage Levi's but never deadstock. The guy I bought them from told me to wash once and never wash again. It got a little stressful with all the crocking, but I would go back to them again and again as they were so comfortable. Over the years, I did wash them a few times when they got totally minging, but the end results were insane. I started to notice the highs and lows – and the fading, it really intrigued me!

'I never found another pair like that, but when Levi's launched Levi's Vintage Clothing, I bought every piece in my style and started the process again, and have been doing so ever since.

'The jacket I'm wearing was a gift from the guys at Post Overalls that I've had for around 12 years. It's one of my favourite jackets. The vest is an old RRL piece in pure indigo with a Wabash stripe. The jeans are from Mister Freedom. I love them – I love the fit, the 14-oz denim and the styling.'

LOREN CRONK

Founder of Loren/BLKSMTH

Shot in Greenpoint, New York

'The hat is our store brand – Loren – which, yes, is my name too. They are made by one of the oldest hat factories left in New York, using Japanese shirting weight 2x1 denim. We also make these in a 10.5-oz Cone blue-black 2x1, using recycled plastic bottles in the fill yarns.

'The jacket is a left-hand twill Wrangler Blue Bell. I'm a big fan of left-hand twills for the velvet-soft hand and the unique way they wear down. This piece is extra special, with nice rusted-out keyholes and shanks, and other rust stains around the jacket.

'The jeans are from my more affordable BLKSMTH line. They are 100 per cent sourced in the US, from the trims and the labels to the Cone denim, and manufactured in Texas. This particular pair is in our Pittsburgh wash. Only 20 pairs were made originally, but there are more to come. Most of our BLKSMTH series is sold raw/unwashed for the wearer to break in themselves, but from time to time we do small-batch washes in something special.'

HERBERT JOHNSON

Creative director of Prospective Flow, LA

Shot at the Liberty Trade Show, New York

'The search for the best denim has been a journey that has introduced me to Japanese craftsmanship and attention to detail. Producing, selling and wearing our products is my way of passing on the passion and spirit of everybody involved in the process.

'I am wearing an oversized indigo-dyed shirt, oversized pants and vest, all by Prospective Flow. I usually like to wear a couple of sizes up for looseness, since denim to me is all about comfort. I layered the vest over the long shirt to add a formal touch.'

OUIGI THEODORE

Creative director of The Brooklyn Circus

Shot in Brooklyn, New York

'I wouldn't consider myself a denim nerd, expert or connoisseur, but I am very particular about my jeans and where they come from. It's all about the fit, the fabric, the brand philosophy and, of course, the almighty cuff – the higher the better.

'I am wearing a pair of Blacksmith jeans by the guys at Rising Sun. They gave them to me as a trial pair because I ordered the line to be sold at our store. I am a huge fan of what they do. They approach the denim craft in a similar way to the Japanese – with real precision and attention to detail. This pair takes me back to the turn of the century, when real men worked in these. They were built to be worn daily under some rough conditions.'

OLU ALEGE

Co-Founder of www.streetlevelculture.com

Shot in New York

'I was born in Brooklyn, raised in the Bronx and grew up on the streets of New York City. I remember wearing Mecca and Tommy jeans as a kid in the '90s. Denim was so huge back then and still is now. It was all about how baggy your jeans were and how you cuffed them: a person wearing high-top sneakers would maybe cuff their denim jeans a bit higher than a person wearing low tops; there were unwritten rules to style. I believe the wash of your denim should complement your sneakers at all times.

New York City street culture is so self-aware and in your face and a part of that translates into who I am today. This denim jumpsuit speaks to me in so many ways, it's a mix of shirt and denim overalls, which were big growing up in New York. I remember playing in the summertime with denim overalls near the fire hydrant. Life was good. I'm not into too many labels or brands, I'd rather have and wear ideas, I think that's what fashion should be.'

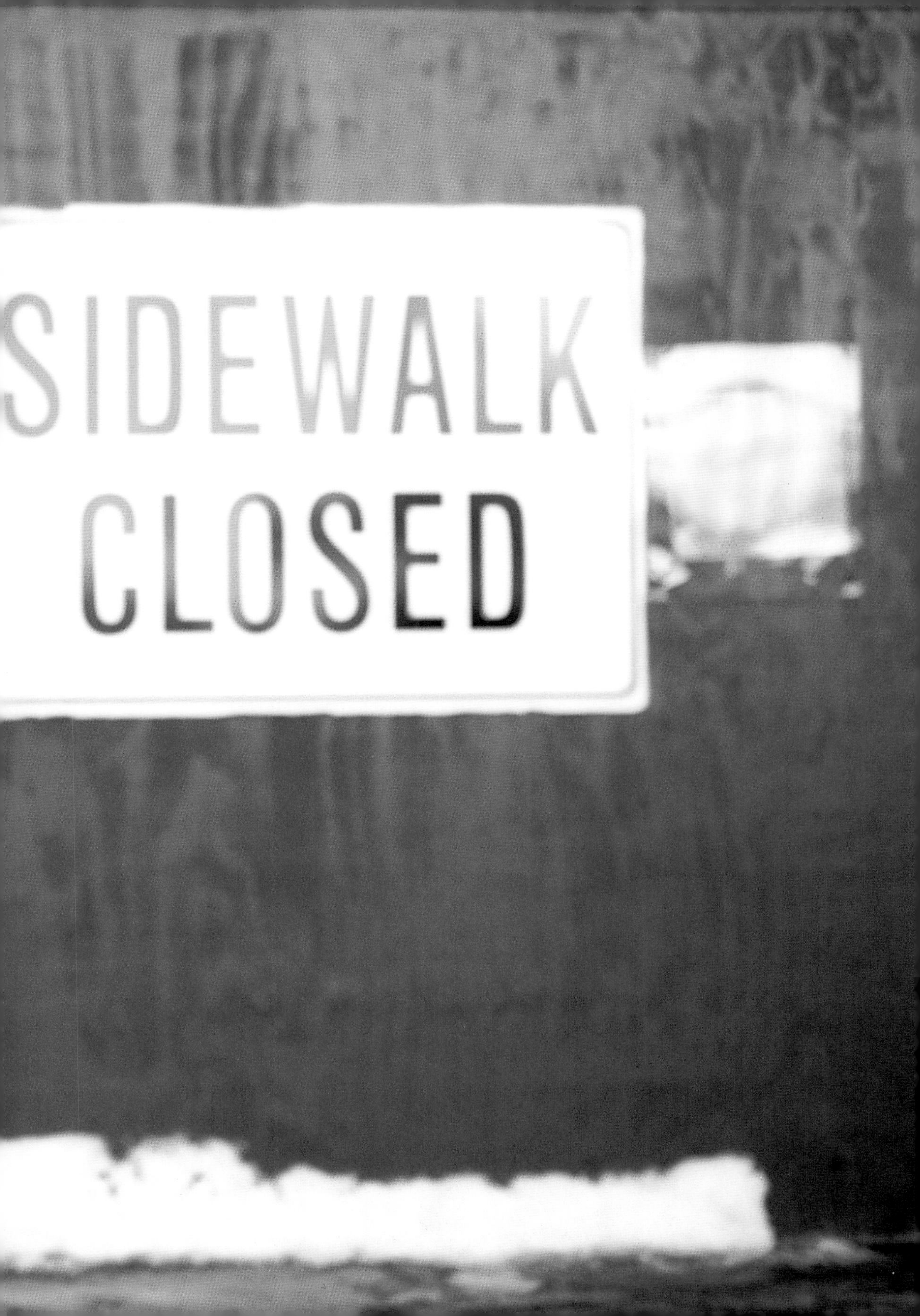
SIDEWALK
CLOSED

RUSSELL MANLEY

Founder of Tommy Guns hair salons

Shot in Brooklyn, New York

'The jacket I'm wearing is a vintage 1940s Lee engineer jacket. I'm a big guy, so finding vintage pieces where the arms are long enough or the chest is big enough is difficult. This jacket fits great. The repro ones aren't quite the same – they lack the worn-in, lived-in feel of old denim.

'The pants are from my favourite denim guys, RRL – the attention to detail they put into everything they make is incredible. The fabric is a replica of a fabric from the 1910s/20s and is indigo-dyed with a discharge print. The chino-ish style comes from a pair of Boss of the Road early work pants.'

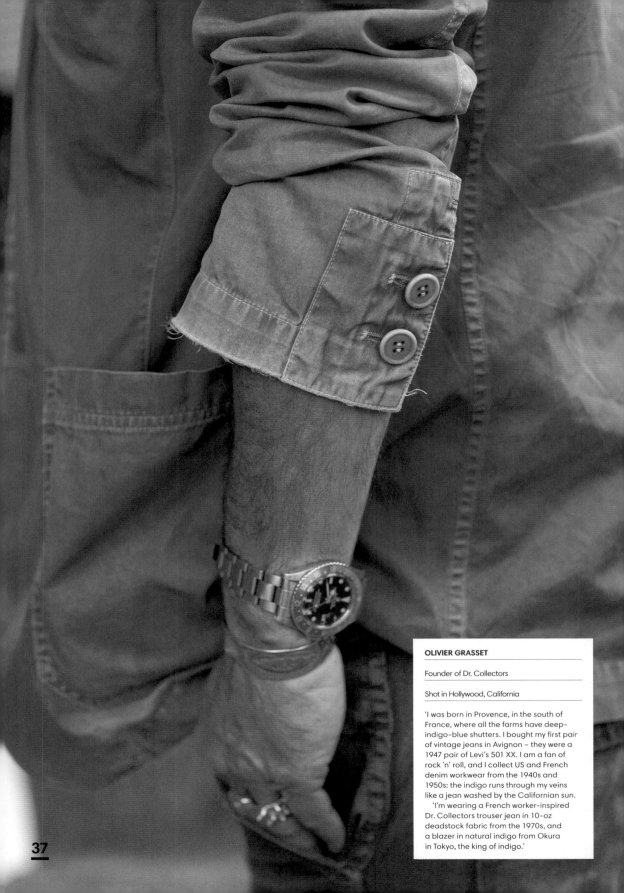

OLIVIER GRASSET

Founder of Dr. Collectors

Shot in Hollywood, California

'I was born in Provence, in the south of France, where all the farms have deep-indigo-blue shutters. I bought my first pair of vintage jeans in Avignon – they were a 1947 pair of Levi's 501 XX. I am a fan of rock 'n' roll, and I collect US and French denim workwear from the 1940s and 1950s: the indigo runs through my veins like a jean washed by the Californian sun.

'I'm wearing a French worker-inspired Dr. Collectors trouser jean in 10-oz deadstock fabric from the 1970s, and a blazer in natural indigo from Okura in Tokyo, the king of indigo.'

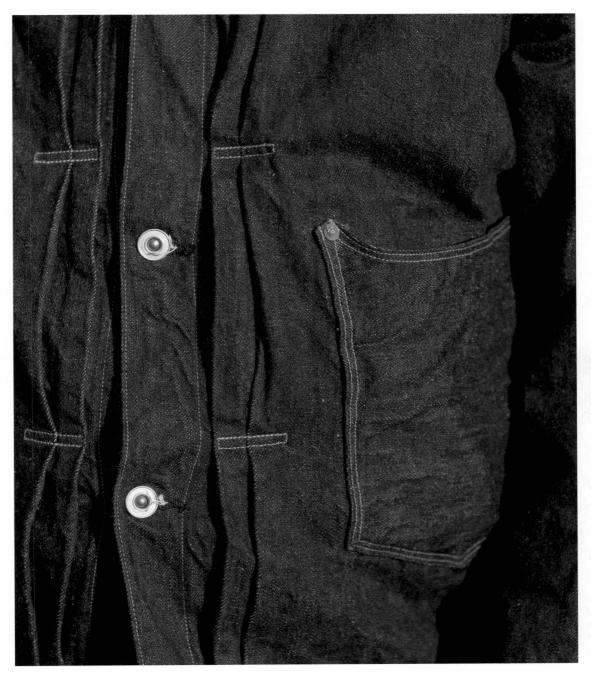

LARRY MCKAUGHAN

Founder of Heller's Cafe, Seattle

Shot at the Rose Bowl Stadium, Pasadena, California

'My style is fairly straightforward. I tend not to wear just vintage or reinterpreted vintage – I prefer to mix and match different periods and styles. It's a purer expression for me.

'My jacket is a Heller's Cafe production piece made in collaboration with Japan's Warehouse company. It's part of our permanent collection. It's one of the first pieces we created, and one of my favourites. It's based on the design of an 1890s Nonpareil work jacket – like a Levi's jacket of the

same period, but from a much more obscure and desirable brand.

'The jeans are 1960s Levi's 501 deadstock. The 501 Big Es are considered transition Levi's. They have some of the characteristics of the earlier indigo Levi's XX, and the later pieces referred to as Big E. I only wear Levi's Big E pants.

'I'll try to wear this pair for a year. They get kind of grungy, but they don't shrink or fade, and they break in perfectly. New or unused denim is always the most collectable and expensive. It's a little extravagant but these are perfect "new-old" and they suit my lifestyle and habits.

'I think of clothing as art, a form of expression; vintage clothing can be used to express what you love and who you are.'

KYLE J. PAK

Owner and designer Homme Boy

Shot in Koreatown, Los Angeles

'The jacket I am wearing is one of my first denim designs. It is a modified version of a trucker jacket, made from five different denim palettes with leather accents, and it is definitely my favourite garment from my first collection.

'As for the jeans, they are a pair of Levi's that I wear almost everyday. I got them in high school and have worn them ever since. I've kept them together with some darning and repair work, and I added some inserts into the side seam to give them a flare.'

44

ZIP STEVENSON

Owner, Hollywood Trading Company

Shot in Los Angeles

'I'm wearing a WWII model of a Sears Hercules Denim Railroad/Barn/Chore/Coverall Jacket. The fact it has so many names is a testament to how versatile the jacket/coat was to so many workers. I found it in a booth of a dealer at the Rosebowl Flea market. What makes it unique and unusual is the way it complied with the War regulations during WWII, so instead of the normal triple stitching on all the seams, the factory only used two stitches to save on thread … also the buttons were generic instead of logo'd.

'The jeans are called Red Cloud. They are a super high-quality pair made in China. What attracted me to them was how heavy and dark blue the selvedge jeans were and the fact they where made at a tiny factory using old American machines. It is the first time Japanese-style jeans have been made there and I am honoured to be the owner of one of the first stores in the US to debut them!'

BRIAN KIM

Founder of THVM Atelier

Shot in Los Angeles

'I've always included a long coat in my wardrobe, as I wear one almost year round. The first garment I ever made was a car coat, when I lived in San Francisco. Denim was the perfect fabric to use because it's durable and can withstand a tactile city. That first coat inspired a fascination with denim and I have made one almost every year since as a tradition.

'With new technologies and finishes from the mills, denim has evolved from utilitarian workwear to offering a much finer, more luxurious level of sophistication. The new weaves and fabric constructions take denim design into categories and garments beyond its traditional uses. I'm not a denim purist and rather enjoy how this timeless fabric evolves yet remains necessary and relevant.

'The seams inside a jean eventually show through to the outside and become part of the overall look. This effect is unique to denim, and is an important part of how a piece ages. I like to eliminate pattern pieces and seams to create a refined structure that will reveal itself over time.'

ADRIANO GOLDSCHMIED

Founder, Genius Group, and designer

Shot in Los Angeles

'The shorter jacket I'm wearing is a vintage Lee made in a canvas loose construction, it's probably mid 1960s. I love the fit and the design, typical of that period, the color, a deep navy blue, is great. It is very comfortable and the shirting pearl snaps are unusual in a jacket. I bought it at the vintage area of American Rag in LA. They have a great selection of vintage.

'The longer-line jacket I bought a few years ago in a small store store in New York near the Mondrian Hotel on Crosby Street. It is new (very unusual for me, as I buy vintage all the time) and

by Swedish brand Denim Demon. I love the fabric; a dark indigo that looks like a wool denim, very particular. The details are great and very well designed, from the buttons with the logo and the quilted chambray as a lining. The fit is very comfortable and it looks like a good traveller jacket.

'My jeans are vintage Jordache that I bought at the Rose Bowl flea market in Pasadena a long time ago, probably 20 years. They are very easy to wear, I wear them rolled up as I hate to make alterations to vintage pieces. The fabric is a beautiful broken twill and the details are nice: the horse embroidery on the coin pocket and the metallic placket on the back pocket, I did a repair by myself a long time ago on the hole on the knee. It's funny as I hated Jordache during their heyday, but now I love them.'

TRAVIS CAINE

Musician (Von Haze, Death In Vegas), artist and woodworker

Shot in Downtown Los Angeles

These jeans are plain old Levi's. I'm sure they made lots of pairs just like these. I've had mine for about 12 years or so. They have slowly deteriorated, and I've kept me ding them with leather, denim and safety pins. It's a pretty crude job but they are still my favourite pair of jeans.

'I bought the jacket around the same time at this grubby little store that used to be on St Marks, East Village, ages ago. I think it was called UK CUNT but it was owned by some Japanese guys. I can't remember … it was so long ago. This jacket was buried under a pile of others like it. As soon as I saw it I knew it would fit perfectly, and it still does to this day. I only started putting the patches on it recently because it's wearing away.'

MIKE HODIS

Founder of Rising Sun & Co.

Shot in Eagle Rock, Los Angeles

'I live and breathe denim and even though I have many options, I find myself gravitating to my ol' trusty Blacksmith jeans which I've been wearing religiously for 14 months without a wash. This is the fit that works best for me, and I wear them with a 4"- double-roll cuff, high-water style. My go-to jacket is the Cattleman. I'm a fan of the waist-length two-pocket-style jackets of old. This one has all the details that I ever wanted, from the angled front yokes to our iconic Acorn pocket shape with the selvedge-reinforced pocket flap detail and the tapered front-pleat detail; it has Rising Sun written all over it. Details and execution is what it's all about, and these two items still look timeless.'

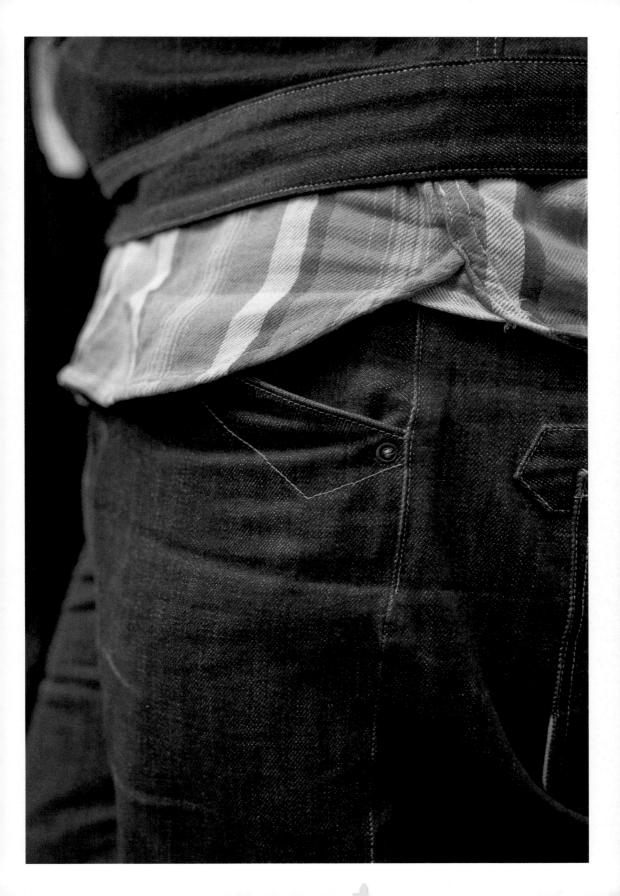

MAURIZIO DONADI

Co-founder of Conduit Creative Office

Shot in Santa Monica, California

'It's hard for me to explain exactly what I do professionally, but I know I have been very lucky to have been involved with some great people on great projects.

'For reasons I can't explain (again), a lot of these projects have somehow involved the colours green and blue. Both colours represent who I am, and these are also the only colours I wear. They both inspire me in different ways. Green calms my fire. Blue inspires me to go deeper.

'The jeans I am wearing are the first prototype of a pair of Levi's 1966 overalls, but with the bib cut off. I have worn them for a few years. They have been repaired many times, always by hand. I am not a collector of vintage jeans, just of great moments.'

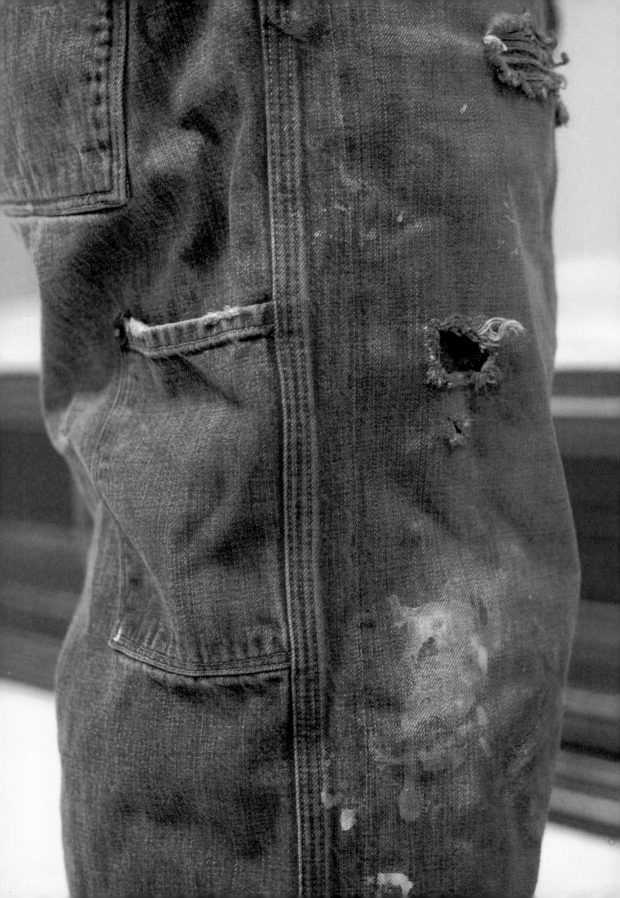

CHRISTOPHE LOIRON

Founder of Mister Freedom

Shot in Los Angeles

'My denim story began in an old army/navy surplus store in the south of France, sometime in the 1970s, where my dad clad me in my first stiff, dark blue raw denim outfit. It was a non-trendy statement – purely functional, sturdy clothes, complete with colourful paper flashers boasting of their longevity and US origins.

'I could dress like the guys in the movies, in the land of rock 'n' roll. Jeans were good enough for Elvis, Eddie Cochran, Steve McQueen, Brando. Denim, man! If it got dirty you'd wash it; if it ripped you'd patch it. This was before all that "vintage look" factory-distressing nonsense. Before things got complicated.

'Fast-forward some 40 years and I'm making my own clothes. The Mister Freedom indigo 14-oz selvedge denim Loco jacket and 12-oz Buckaroos waist overalls I'm wearing were both manufactured in small batches in Los Angeles.

'Simple denim outfits take me back to that childhood comfort zone. They're perfect for when I need to focus on what I'm doing rather than what I'm wearing. I'm not obsessed with cool 'whiskers', I just enjoy the journey. Dark blue denim works for me.'

BENJAMIN PHILLIPS

Co-founder Lot, Stock & Barrel

Shot in Santa Monica, California

'Ever since venturing into the perpetual depths and life-altering journey of collecting and buying vintage denim, I have become obsessed with the progression of density and weights of the fabric itself: 10 oz, 12 oz, 14 oz after soaks. I have become fixated on pushing the limits of the denim weight that one can wear, and for how long. The 1954 14-oz 501s can no longer satiate my undying thirst for heavier denim. Can I sustain comfort and functionality while wearing a densely woven black 21-oz Japanese selvedge denim vest and jean in the sweltering California heat? Yes! Yes, I can.

'This Iron Heart jean and vest have survived 110-degree barbecues, travelled through Europe, Asia and the Americas, were on my side shooting shotguns in the Washington Mountains with my ranching friend Ronnie, and also saved my legs in a chopper collision with a Camaro on Sunset Boulevard, all without even breaking a thread. At a full year of wear, they have barely even begun to fade to a warm grey.'

KEN ITO

CEO of a SF Bay Area assisted-living facility

Shot at the Inspiration LA show, Long Beach

'I used to work for a big farm-export company who compressed big 150-lb bales of hay. I used to load the bales on and off the truck and this is the denim apron I wore while doing that. All the wear you see on it is from that time. I'm not in that business anymore, but I have kept it all this time and wear it for purist denim occasions like these.

'The jeans are pretty special too. My friend Jonathan runs the Bandanna Almanac website; he was at the Kapital Century Denim release night, and got a pair for me. They were actually customized by the president of Kapital, so they are a particularly rare jean.'

KIYA BABZANI

Co-founder of Self Edge

Shot in San Francisco

'I've always been a firm believer that your clothing should tell your story. I wanted to open a store where the clothing had soul, and every garment or accessory not only told a story but took on a story of its own with regular wear.

'I grew up in San Francisco in the 1980s, hence the denim Oakland Athletics hat I'm wearing.

The jacket is a collaboration we did with Iron Heart. It started out as an 18-oz unsanforized indigo denim that was then overdyed black and stitched with cotton/polycore thread so that the contrast stitching would stay somewhat yellow.

'The jeans are by Stevenson Overall Co. They're the only single-needle-stitched production jean in the world, and were inspired by designs from the 1930s, before belt-looping, chainstitching and bar-tacking machines were invented or used widely in factories. The shoes are natural indigo-dyed Visvim sneakers with a persimmon-dyed leather toe-box.'

BART SIGHTS

Director of Global Development, Levi's / Eureka Lab

Shot at Levi's San Francisco

'I'm wearing my treasured Levi's blanket-lined Trucker (see page 80). I traded a cowboy a brand new pair of 501s for this Trucker in a saloon in Big Horn, Wyoming many years ago. It had the army patch on it, and I never took it off. He and I agreed that the blanket-lined Levi's Trucker is the most functional piece of apparel ever.

'The jean is called the Barton. My sister and brother-in-law lovingly made me these pants, and named the model after me. They come from their small, personal, and very extraordinary brand called Imogene+Willie. I have worn them with love, and never washed them.

'My Levi's Sawtooth Shirt is, in my opinion, the most iconic shirt ever. Mine is a prototype that we made with a customized rounded collar. It makes me feel original, but a bit fancy, whenever I wear it.

'The 101st Airborne designed these Corcoran boots, specifically for the night they jumped onto Utah Beach to save the world. Mine are from Corcoran, the original maker, and I have worn through three soles over the past 20 years.

'I have always worn a neck kerchief, whether hot or cold. This one is from Isabel Marant, and I have worn it until the shibori print has turned to holes.'

JONATHAN LUKACEK

Founder of the Bandanna Almanac, Osaka

Shot in Denim Bruin, San Francisco

'This Lee jacket was in rough condition when I bought it; the way I like my vintage. I don't care about the label or the age, just the condition. The more destroyed, stained and repaired a garment is, the more I like it. After these pictures were taken I had it repaired and modified further by a friend.

'The jeans are Kapital Century Denim. I've been wearing them almost everyday for a year and a half, and I machine-wash them every couple of months. The fades have come and gone as I'm always adding coats of persimmon tannin to them to get a more interesting colour fade. They've been incredibly tough and reliable jeans for me, and are by far my favourite pair.'

NICK KEMP

Co-owner of Jack/Knife Outfitters

Shot in San Francisco

'Everything I'm wearing, with the exception of my dad's vintage US Navy sweater, was made by me. The vest is a limited-edition collaboration piece we did with Tellason in our first year of business. Almost everything I wear is made by me for me, apart from some vintage pieces, hats and shoes.'

JOHN ALBURL

Co-owner of Jack/Knife Outfitters

Shot in San Francisco

'Most of us in this book are probably going to look like blue people from a distance. Hopefully readers will be in-the-know enough to tell us apart!

'Almost everyone I know has their "I wear this everyday" ensemble. The set of clothes that I am wearing in this picture has been my go-to for a while now. I'm wearing a beanie, an indigo-dyed terry cloth western snap shirt, my custom Jack/Knife jeans and my workboots. I am very lucky to be able to say that my jeans were custom-made for me by Nick [Kemp, page 86], my business partner at Jack/Knife.'

90

Europe

Europe is the melting pot of numerous denim styles and personalities, its eclectic palette of 'de Nîmes' is unrivalled. Europe weaves its rich history into every jean, but adds a little here and there to create something quirky and spirited. Europe is home to the British anarchists of the denim scene, fuelled by biker gangs, punk rockers and Camden metalheads. Across the water the eccentric Parisians use their artistic flair and avant-garde energy to spawn such diverse labels as the legendary Marithé et François Girbaud and the rock 'n' roll April77. Travelling south, you'll find the world renowned Italian denim masters, laundry experts and laboratory dwellers who put Diesel, Gas and Fiorucci on the map in the late 1970s. But head north and the scene changes pace again: the denim-heads are out in full force in Berlin or Amsterdam, where devoted blue-bloods hang out, where the stores look like denim temples and it's a wonder the canals don't run indigo. And who could miss out Scandinavia, a region that showcases some of the most modern and effortlessly stylish denim brands of recent history: where the greyer skies have inspired all levels of the market from the achingly hip Acne through to the more purist Unionville and Nudie.

DAVE CARROLL

Owner of Pride & Clarke / La Rocka! co-collaborator

Shot in London

'The blanket-lined Lee Storm Rider jacket I'm
wearing is one I acquired over ten years ago,
when I was a vintage clothes dealer at London's

Portobello Market. I'd always wanted one of these
after seeing Kirk Douglas wear one in a 1950s film.
It's an excellent layering piece for when I'm out on
the bikes.

  'I've teamed the jacket with a 1958 pair of Levi's
Capital Es. I found these the day after proposing
to my beautiful fiancée in Paris last year. They're
from a Sunday market in the Marais. It was a
great weekend!'

SHAKA MAIDOH

Co-founder of Art Comes First

Shot in London

'So these jeans are limited-edition Levi's. I can't remember the name because I've had them 10 or 12 years. A friend working at Levi's at the time bought them for my birthday; I liked them so much I went back and got a second pair that same day. I usually buy things in pairs if I like them, and this was a good decision: a few friends saw them just weeks later and went to get some but they were sold out. I'm not sure they've been reissued since.

'I had both pairs altered differently. The first I made into a carrot shape as that's what I was into at that time. My good friend Sam helped me alter the second pair, which are what I'm wearing here. This alteration was quite complex, as they were taken in not from the sides but from the front. I left the length the same, so I can play around with that as I wear them. I believe these are a one-of-a-kind piece, and having two pairs means these ones still look new even though they're over 10 years old. The second pair are worn out now!'

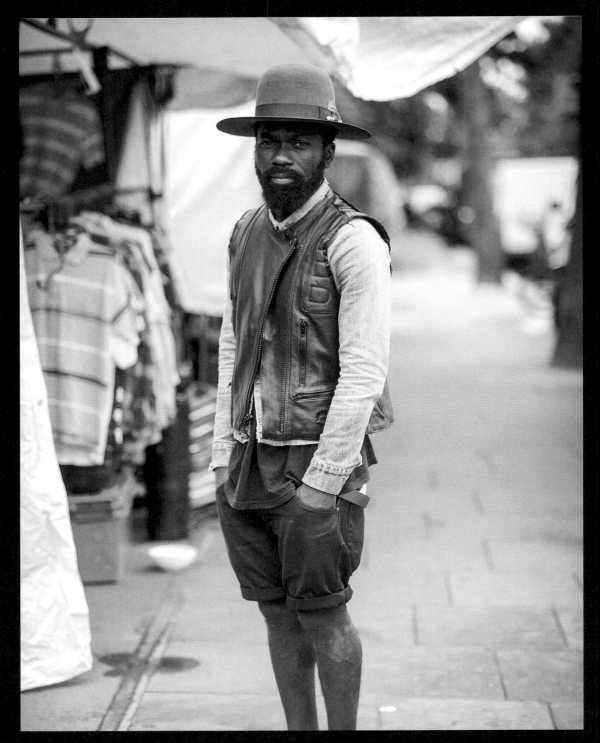

SAM LAMBERT

Co-founder of Art Comes First

Shot in London

'Since my background is in tailoring, I customize every vintage piece I wear; it's nice to keep things alive with a new touch. The denim jacket that I'm wearing in these pictures is a vintage Lee jacket that I altered by trimming the collar, sleeves, body and length.

'The leather vest is a motorbike jacket from Akito that I customized to fit my denim look. For me, denim goes with leather, and vice versa – it's the perfect marriage.

'The black wax denim shorts are from a pair of Ozwald Boateng pants. Since they came from a tailoring brand they already fitted well, but I cut them to shorts and fitted the legs.'

DOUG GUNN

Co-founder of The Vintage Showroom

Shot in London

'One of the hardest things for me in our business is retaining my wardrobe. Although our showroom is some 5,000 square feet, with pieces from around the world, more often than not it's the wash on my jeans, the detail on my belt, the stitching on my jacket that a customer wants. Over the years I have regretfully sold many things literally off my back, but sometimes bills have to be paid.

'The denim smock I'm wearing is one I've fought to retain; it's a 1920s US Army denim pullover with zinc buttons. I've had it from pretty much raw, so the wash and fade is all me. If you see me wearing it, it's not for sale!

'The jeans are the last of a batch I found in a sale in the US – all 1950s Big E Levi's. Whoever the last owner was, they were all my size. For a vintage dealer I am a shameful user of vintage jeans – I wear them to death. Our repair guy always flags pairs that have just one repair left in them. The scarf is a Japanese indigo print fabric that a friend bought for me. The music in the background was Miles. It was a blue day!'

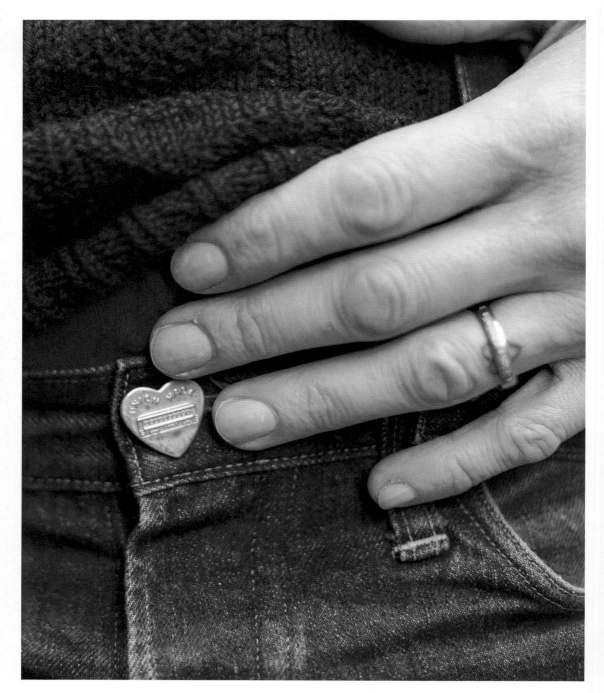

MARK WESTMORELAND

Owner of The One Goods

Shot in Air Street, London

'My jeans are a prototype for 'The One Slim'. The cut is based on a cross-section of Wrangler, Lee and Levi's jeans used in spaghetti westerns, (we narrowed the hem by an inch for the production). They were rinsed before they were worn and have been worn daily for seven months, with one more wash during that time.

'Again, my jacket was rinsed before being worn and has been worn for five months. The cotton is from three states in the US – then dyed and woven in Japan. The construction and cast is based on a 1930s Levi's banner. It's a compilation of what I consider to be the very best of many vintage jackets I have owned over the years.

'My jumper is an Eriskay fisherman's jumper, it's knitted on circular needles so there are no seams. It took my dad over a year to knit. He gave it to me for Christmas 2010 – never has a gift from my dad meant so much.

'The Post Office bag is the same age as I am – from 1969. I wish I was looking this fresh!

'I believe in buying things and wearing things that are designed with love and made with pride.'

RUDY RUPEN BUDHDEO

CEO of Son of a Stag & JFK 1993

Shot in London

'The blank canvas of a raw, unsanforized denim is an exciting thing for me. The jeans and jean jacket that I am wearing are by Warehouse/Heller's Cafe and were a gift from my good friends Ichiro-San and the Warehouse brothers.

'Wearing these denims celebrates another episode of friendship and I look forward to wearing the jeans for many years to come – evoking memories of a great relationship with the Warehouse organization.

'I wore both pieces in the bath, but ended up soaking the jacket at a higher temperature, as the shrink was not enough the first time. This instability is the beauty of a great denim.

'The jeans are a great replica of pants as they were around 1870 to 1910: a straight fit using 13-oz denim, constructed in Japan with a fabric waistband label, all single-needle construction, oxidized rivets, a continuous fly and a crotch reinforcement – simply a benchmark jean.

'I am also wearing the matching jacket by Warehouse/Heller's Cafe, and a Spellbound shirt. Spellbound by the Domingo group are friends of mine who have hosted numerous factory visits and many special meals for me. Spellbound is generally my personal favourite when it comes to shirts.'

HENRY HOLLAND

Founder of House of Holland

Shot in London

'So these are my favourite jeans by Ksubi: they are the only brand I wear and the fit is called Van Winkle. Whenever I go to Australia I pick some up, and with these ones I've kinda worn them to death and then cut the hem down. I always like to work with some denim every season. From really early on we collaborated with Levi's and did two seasons with them. That then led to us doing our own. I love working with denim, and we're working on launching our own denim line next season.'

HUGGY LEAVER

Caretaker, actor and voiceover artist

Shot in London

'As you can see, I'm wearing a Type II Levi's jacket that I have patched up with various bike patches and thread. It's really got that early 1970s vibe going on, along with my '61 Econoline pick-up truck and sandals by Vans. The jeans are Levi's 201s, 1933-cut White Label. I just love old bikes, cars and denim – what else is there, daddy-o? PS: the retro Harley chopper is on its way…'

MOHSIN SAJID

Owner / Creative director of Endrime

Shot in London

My first memories as a child were the hum of my mother's Industrial Lockstitch machine. Coming from a big family and being one of the youngest, having to prove myself is something that's built into my DNA. It's for this reason I've always enjoyed difficult tasks, from complicated pattern-cutting to drawings. I guess it stems from Islamic design - a complicated, clean aesthetic that in the end turns into something beautiful. This is what keeps me unique from the rest. I feel denim workwear is still unrealized. I enjoy pushing workwear garments into a new, modern and dynamic direction, but still keeping the overall aesthetic clean with a purest approach in terms of fabrics and construction. There is a deep passion in me to learn and gain knowledge in denim design, from every aspect – and for me it's exciting, I always feel I'm scratching the surface.

FERGADELIC

Co-founder of Aries Denim

Shot in London

'I'm not a denimhead, but I wear jeans all the
time. I'm wearing jeans from Supreme; they're
good quality and shape, made in the United States
and have no big branding or horrible wash 'n'
wear. The vest has two patches, one vintage (the
panther), which I added hand-stitched embroidery
to, saying "Clans Of The Alphane Moon", which is
my favourite Philip K. Dick book. The other patch
is from a cool eBay store that makes custom
patches. My denim jacket is hand-embroidered
by me with the names of my fave Thrash/Crossover
bands … plus the killer Bad Boy Club dude, which
is my favourite Logo of all time.'

ÖRJAN ANDERSSON

Founder of Weekday, Cheap Monday and
Örjan Andersson

Shot in Stockholm

'My outfit is chosen from what I prefer to
wear right now. The denim jacket was the
first garment I ever designed. It was for my
Weekend [later Weekday] store and I made it
in 2001 in black denim. I bleached the jacket
with chlorine at my local laundry at that time.
One of my neighbours had left a sweater
there and because I was not careful enough
I spilled some chlorine on it too. I had to buy
him a new one, but it was worth it for the
result on my jacket.

'The jeans I'm wearing are from my Örjan
Andersson brand, and the name of the pant
is Unisex Shifting Black, from the Autumn
2013 collection. The fit is tight, with a normal
high waist and almost straight legs. The
fabric is from Swift Denim, with some stretch
and acid-wash effects. The bleached denim
shirt is from the Örjan Andersson Spring
2013 collection.

'I have a brand slogan that uses the first
and last letters of the Swedish alphabet,
which are also my initials: "Från Ö Till A."
It means you can make the same thing in
multiple ways, which is what denim design
is all about.'

HAKIM KRIM

Guitarist and singer of Dead Lord

Shot in Stockholm

'Being a semi-broke rocker, Cheap Monday jeans are a lifesaver. They look good and are dirt cheap to get here in Stockholm.

'These are probably my favourites. I think I even got them at an employee's discount when I worked some extra hours at a jeans store. They've been patched up way too many times. I've worn them on loads of gigs, slept in them, and spilled lots of beer and whatnot on them. And of course I've never washed them, apart from hosing them off whenever they got too smelly. However, at the time of writing, they are unfortunately dead. They split mid-crotch while doing some power knee-slides in Helsinki. But I'm keeping them for patching future ones.

'The jacket is an old 1960s Wrangler that I got on eBay. It's way too small for me to be able to button it up, but too-small denim jackets look way better unbuttoned.'

AXEL NYHAGE

CEO of The Local Firm

Shot in Stockholm

'When Richard Hutchinson and I started to talk about The Local Firm our discussions always revolved around fashion and the way jeans looked and felt during the late 1980s and early '90s. That feeling of when open-end 14-oz jeans were standard, and people were laying on their backs on the floor fighting to get their hips into slim-fits. When Sean Penn and Madonna were the original star couple, and when you went to the movies just to see the Levi's launderette commercial. With The Local Firm we want to capture that original fashion-jeans feeling using contemporary fits and reinterpreting the 1980s/90s fabrics – and surrounding the denim with garments that complete that feeling and look.

'Here I'm wearing a sort of signature The Local Firm look. The jeans are made from a specially developed fixed 13.75-oz black, open-end denim that we developed with one of our denim weavers the very first season – Autumn 2008 – and have kept in the collection ever since.'

KLAS ERIXON

Founder of Pace Jeans

Shot in Stockholm

'I am thankful to life and my dad that I got into a pair of denim jeans at two years old in 1962. My whole life since then has been about denim. All my outfits have a history and are a reflection of my daily life. I've been wearing dry denim jackets and jeans since before you could even buy washed denim in Sweden. My history of living the blue life has a perspective of many years.

'The jacket that I am wearing is a Pace jacket with a unique fabric. It's an exact early 1940s re-make from Japan and uses the same water-resistant canvas used by the army during World War II. The chambray work shirt has a history dating back to the early 1900s.

'My Premium Pace jeans in a classic early 1960s fit are new friends that I am getting to know. This selvedge-denim pair will carry my personal history and be a part of my everyday life for some years. They will retire as denim art on my wall.

'Denim is my life. I was born into it and I will leave this life in a pair of jeans.'

CARL MALMGREN

Head of denim design at Cheap Monday

Shot in Stockholm

'I don't overly respect a vintage item if it's
something that I want to wear. I think it's
more interesting to turn an old worn item
into something of your own. The customizing
tradition in denim is very appealing, and you
should experiment and bring old garments
to life by using your imagination: patching,
tinting, decorating and altering the fit really
adds a layer to the story of a garment.

'My vintage Levi's jacket is from some
random second-hand store. I tinted it
in a homemade dye of coffee, tea and
some other stuff to make it less crisp in
tone, and I cut the collar into a V shape
to update the look a bit.

'My jeans are a Cheap Monday fit called
High Slim, which we introduced for A/W
2013. It's slim but non-stretch. This one is
also cropped with a raw edge.'

ELIAS JUBRAN

Sales ambassador for Levi's Nordics

Shot in Stockholm

'So far I've had two life-changing moments: the first was hearing Iron Maiden for the first time; the second was when I put on a pair of women's jeans. I realized that I could get clothes just as tight and perfectly fitted for me as anyone else. The feeling that the clothes you are wearing are custom-tailored for you – that was my epiphany (and what made me want to work with denim).

'These jeans are Levi´s Slight Curve Straight, which are made for women without a butt. The denim jacket is my workhorse, my uniform. It's a Levi´s women's trucker that I've been wearing for the last four years. It's never been washed. Regardless of whether I'm at a death metal show, an uptight business meeting or just cleaning out my basement, it's there.

'I believe in buying clothes with great quality but cheap enough for you to dare to live in them! They look better after years of careless messing around, and this jacket is my proof. It's even started to tear in the armpits because of the salty creases left by four years of Viking sweat.'

JOHAN LINDSTEDT

Fabric and finish designer at Nudie Jeans

Shot in Gothenburg

'I'm wearing a second-hand biker jacket which I almost never take off; it has a tailored feeling and fits like a glove! Under that I have a black hoodie and tee from a really small brand working exclusively with organic cotton.

'The denims are rigid indigo with black coating so the indigo will shine through after wear and tear, giving them an almost midnight shine. I always go for unwashed denim as I like the look during the whole process. Being very analogue, your jeans almost record your memories: "this scratch comes from that party", and so on – like a vinyl record in a way.'

REY GAUTIER

Creative director of Edwin, Europe

Shot in the Vosges Mountains, France

'I count myself fortunate to be able to work in the way that I do. My life revolves around my passions, which effectively have, over time, become my work, my family and my home. Living where we do, which is relatively isolated, I tend to favour practical garments suited to the environment as I spend a lot of time outdoors. Denim is always at the core of this.

'My jeans are Edwin Japan 50s, which have taken a battering over the years. I have a few pairs in various stages of life, abuse and continued repair, as they remain my personal favourite cut. The jacket is an old Edwin western. A few years ago, I swapped with a friend who had worn this under his leather while riding motorcycles for years, which has created unique wear patterns and unusual fading. This is why I love heavy denim. It allows me to just live and not really think about clothing; I'm free to move from one activity to another seamlessly.'

BRICE PARTOUCHE

Studio director and founder of April77

Shot in Paris

'I like to wear my jeans a bit too short – probably because that's how I saw and still see my dad wearing his. He's a denim dude too. I don't remember why I cropped them like this, but I guess I was too lazy to make a proper hem, or maybe it was my reaction to those preppy denim guys looking too perfect and boring…

'These are my favourite April77 jeans (I only have two pairs – these indigos and some in black. I'll wear them until they're dead). The fit is called Dictator and of course they were raw two years ago.

'My jacket is a classic black April77 trucker-style jacket. I customized it with some of my favourite black metal and thrash metal bands patches. Jeff Hanneman of Slayer died just the day before these shots were taken, so this is my tribute to one of the best metal bands ever! I might sound like a teenager, but I've been into heavy metal since I was 11 and I still dig it.'

KATSU MANABE

International sales director Japan Blue Group

Shot in Paris

'I was born in Kurashiki (near Kojima, Okayama, in Japan) and have worked for Japan Blue Group for around 12 years. Growing up, I was just a normal guy: interested in fashion, food, music, sport… not really interested in my father's denim business until I realized what he had done with the Japanese denim market in the 1990s.

'These jeans are my masterpiece: Momotaro 1005SP, 15.7-oz GTB ("going to battle") in deep indigo selvedge Zimbabwe cotton. The wear is four years. I washed them for the first time after five months. The second wash was three months later, and since then I have washed them whenever they get smelly or dirty! This jean fits my body perfectly and is the most comfortable heavy-ounce denim in my collection.

'The vest is by Rampuya (part of Japan Blue Group). It's a yarn-dyed natural indigo, woven using vintage shuttle looms into a fabric called Kasuri, an ancient Japanese fabric once produced by hand loom.'

FRANÇOIS GIRBAUD

Designer

Shot at Denim by Première Vision in Paris

'Jeanswear doesn't have to mean indigo or a workwear attitude, which was the case when the garment had to adapt to the lifestyle of the wearer. For instance, I don't wear cowboy or work boots anymore since there are no longer cacti in the city!

'I am not especially drawn to animals and yet I have observed cattle over a long time and am intrigued and inspired by them. So the pants I am wearing are inspired by the way the hoof and leg are attached.

'They are made in a multiweave fabric that delineates areas without having to make any unnecessary cuts. The trainer and pant leg are united in the ankle hole, emphasizing ankle signage, which has been somewhat forgotten these days as jeans are too often rolled up.

'My Dior redingote [long coat] looks very OK Corral with my feathered scarf. I haven't climbed high enough to sport an eagle on my big head yet…'

PHILIP RUDJEANSKI

Denim designer and founder of BALAGANS

Shot at Denim by Première Vision, Paris

'As a designer and craftsman I design, sew and wash my jeans, and of course I wear them too.

'The denim designs I am wearing here are from BALAGANS, the denim couture project I established with a colleague in 2010. These pieces are from the first experimental denim collection, "Who's Wearing the Trousers?", inspired by harbour workers, their posture and lifestyle. The idea was to tell a story through clothes – full of humour, clichés and irony.'

MILES JOHNSON

Head of Levi's Vintage Clothing

Based in Amsterdam, shot in Paris

'The Levi's 501 jeans I'm wearing are from the 1950s. When I bought them they'd hardly been worn and, as I am an impatient type, I gave them to my friend Dennis to wear them in. He works in a plastics factory near where I live in the UK. He wore them to work almost every day for a year and got small spots of plastic and paint on them, which I later removed with solvents and sandpaper. They are one of my favourite pairs, which I've been wearing in more over the last five years. They just keep getting better. Every time they rip, pick or unravel, I stitch and patch them up. I'm determined to have these jeans for the rest of my life, and pass them on to someone else.

'The sleeveless Levi's trucker vest is an old Orange Tab that has been customized and ripped; in places it only has parts of the seam to hold it together. I bought it at the Rose Bowl flea market in Pasadena, near LA. It was my favourite shopping experience of all time. I'm always looking for old denim garments that have had something done to them that makes them more interesting and unlike everyone else's.

'The scarf I printed myself in Jaiphur, India. I printed it with mud on Kahdi cotton, and overdyed it with natural indigo. It's 5 metres long, but it's so thin I can fold it in three before wrapping it around my neck. I love all the pale shades of natural indigo, when they become a grey/green version of sky blue.'

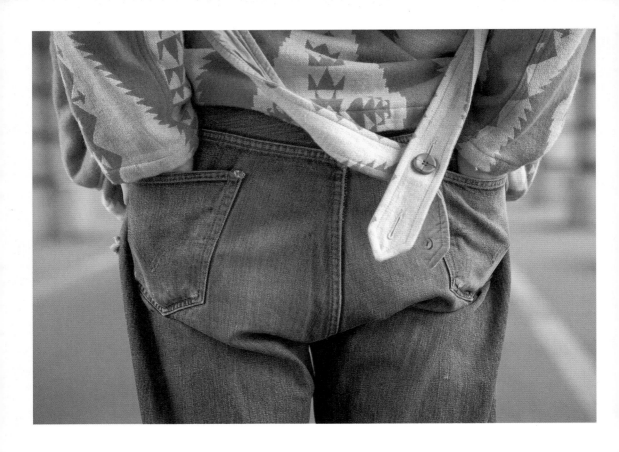

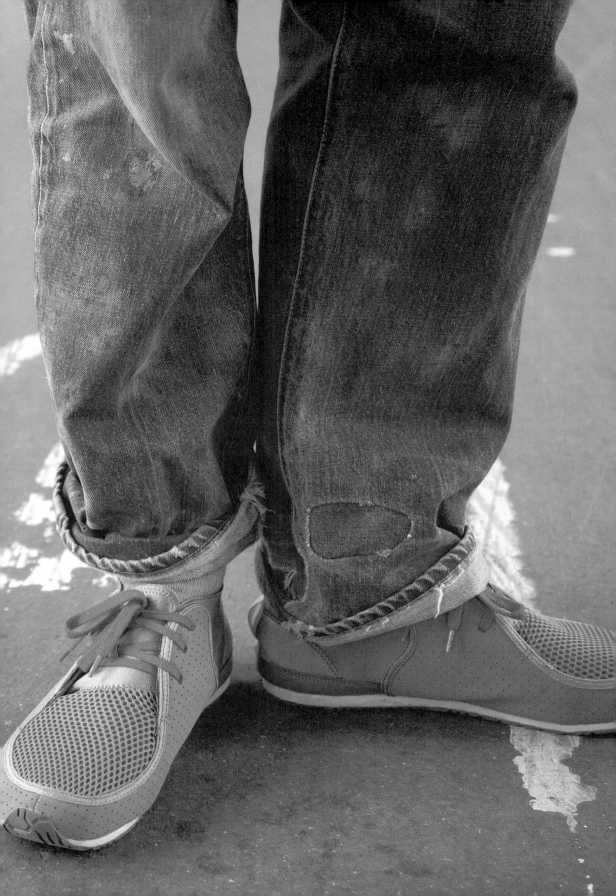

RENÉ STROLENBERG

Co-founder & commercial director Tenue de Nîmes

Shot in Amsterdam

'My jeans are a custom pair made especially for me by our friend and "denim artist" Koen Tossijn at Atelier Tossijn. We co-created my ideal denim pattern and this is the result, made by hand at Koen's atelier in Amsterdam from a 14.75- oz Kuroki fabric. My vest and shirt are made by Double RL. We are one of the few stores in the world to carry this exclusive line by Ralph Lauren. The legend is that Ralph Lauren himself hand-picks the stores that are allowed to sell this Double RL – a line that was created as a modern tribute to the independent spirit of the untamed West and the American blue-collar worker. Everything we love about jeans and its timeless, effortless style is captured in the Double RL brand.'

JASON DENHAM

Founder of Denham the Jeanmaker

Shot in Amsterdam

'I've worn jeans all my life; they are my style choice, my passion and my hobby. For 20 years I have obsessively collected denim and everything that goes with it, and I'm lucky that I have turned this in to my day job! I designed my first jean at university in England and I haven't looked back since.

'First the jeans. I am wearing a five-pocket Denham model called Grade, naturally worn in for three years and handwashed five times. They're made from 12.5-oz Japanese selvedge virgin (raw), which is my favourite cloth to wear in.

'The jacket is our Mao style. It's a worker jacket, part inspired by Chinese and French workwear, with signature collar scissors. The shirt is a blue oxford Pin model, with an indigo pique tie.

'It's blue all the way for me, except a flash of colour on my Jack Purcells – they're Hudson Bay limited editions.'

PIERRE MORISSETTE

Creative director, G-Star Raw

Shot in Amsterdam

'My passion for functional clothing started very early in life, it was inspired by uniforms rather than fashion. Finding army clothing and deadstock workwear was, and still is, a kick. This passion resulted in a number of stores and my own label. Twenty-five years ago I was asked to collaborate on the development of a modern jeanswear brand; today I am still with G-Star and it's the most fantastic project in my career.

'I'm wearing the G-Star Elwood, the very first 3D denim which we introduced in 1996. At the time, 5-pockets were everywhere and we wanted to create the denim of the future: modern and new. For me this jeans represents our commitment to innovating in denim.'

MENNO VAN MEURS

Co-founder and CEO Tenue de Nîmes

Shot in Amsterdam

'Although I own many jeans there are very few that come close to the feeling of a vintage Levi's 501. This particular treasure is a late-1970s pair. The beauty of it is that it was already heavily beaten up when I bought it. So, with time and wear, I kept repairing the jeans myself. I used spare denim material for the larger damaged areas and several pieces of natural indigo fabric from Japan to cover up the small rips and tears. The vintage selvedge denim that completes the outfit is a jacket by JC Penney. It symbolises forgotten times in which people (even at the commercial brands) would actually take time to make products that would last a lifetime. The coat is a vintage piece by Pendleton.'

OLAF HUSSEIN

Founder of Olaf Hussein

Shot in Amsterdam

'The long wool coat I'm wearing is a clean, simple and elegant coat that suits any style and almost every occasion. I like to style it with my vintage Levi's jacket that I bought last month at Spitalfields Market in London. It's in a beautiful washed-out shade with frayed collar and small holes forming from natural wear. The jeans I'm wearing are my signature denim jeans, made from 13-oz. sanforized selvedge denim that's been dyed with natural indigo and sourced from the Kuroki mill in Okayama, Japan. I have been wearing this pair for about 10 months straight with only one wash, and I just love the strong fading, wear patterns and patina. The hand-painted sneakers are a collaboration between Converse and Margiela. The idea of the paint is that it will eventually wear off, creating a unique patina on the shoe: very cool. I just love wearing classic garments with a clean modern design that are easy to combine and long lasting in both style and quality. I am a big believer in buying good things, and owning them a long time!'

TONY TONNAER

Founder of Kings of Indigo

Shot in Amsterdam

'I'm a sucker for everything Americana and fresh Japanese style. I started Kings of Indigo so that I could mix the two passions together.

'On this very sunny, brisk day in Amsterdam, I wore an old Levi's bleached chambray shirt, a Mister Freedom indigo vest and my favourite jacket – a 1998 RRL baseball jacket with the softest leather sleeves ever. I'm wearing it with a boro scarf, made from old kimonos and bought in Nakameguro in Tokyo.

'Of course I'm wearing my favourite K.O.I denims, – the Louis model – made from 14-oz Collect denim with recycled weft. It's started to break in nicely. The watch is a 1974 Rolex submariner. I inherited it from my dad; he bought it when my mum left him, to deal with the loss. The silver bracelet and the Dalai Lama blessed red rope were from two of my best friends.'

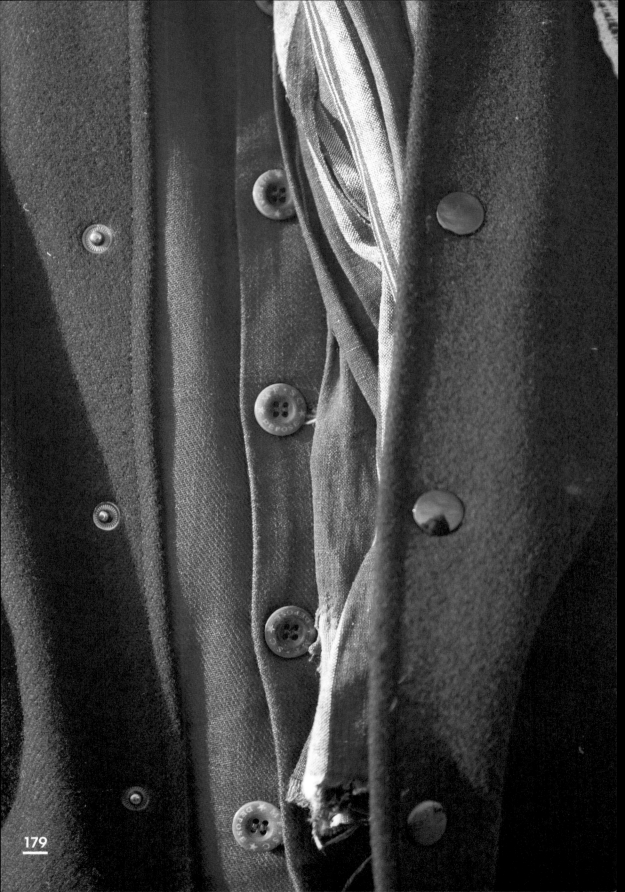

ROB HARMSEN

Co-founder of Eat Dust, Antwerp

Based in Antwerp, shot in LA

'The pants I'm wearing are our new-fit 76 which is a boot cut and my favourite pant. The jacket is our fit 673. All the denim we use is from Kurabo and is a 13 3/4oz blue selvedge. The jacket is the 673B, blanket-lined with a deadstock 60-year-old Belgian army wool. We only made 80 of them and all of them have a custom label inside with the number and name of the store or person who bought it. For FW14 we found a 35-year-old green army wool and used it to make three of our styles. We like to find old fabrics and use them for our garments. The scarf is one from a collaboration we did with David Spencer in London.'

DANIEL WERNER

Store manager at 14 oz.

Shot in Berlin

'I was into skateboarding as a teenager. My first jeans were pretty baggy, but good enough to do everything I wanted on my board. They eventually became more and more narrow, but I still wear them pretty low.

'I then discovered Japanese denim, which introduced me to the history of denim, the different qualities, the idea of breaking in raw denim and giving it your own character. From then on, I wasn't able to buy washed denim anymore. My wardrobe is full of raw denims made in the US or Japan.

'These are natural indigo-dyed jeans, made from Japanese fabric by Dutch brand Denham. I love the way they fade. Denham take pretty old-school, high-quality fabrics but give them a modern, up-to-date cut, something you often miss with the traditional big denim brands.'

ALJOSCHA AUGUSTIN

Co-owner of Fein und Ripp

Shot in Berlin

'To be honest, my passion for heritage style is still in its infancy. It all goes hand in hand with the opening of our family business, Fein und Ripp, with my brother and father [see following pages]. From this moment on I developed a keen interest in garments generally.

'The undershirt introduced me to the good old style. This one is a deadstock piece that's 90 years old; it was woven on a circular knitting machine in the 1920s in West Germany. We found a huge stock of them in 2009 in an abandoned garment factory in the Swabian Alps.

'Then when we discovered the young German brand Pike Brothers, our love for denim caught fire. That's why I'm wearing a 1958 Roamer Pant and 1952 Rider Shirt from this marvellous company. No big surprise that we sell their stuff in our store as well, right?'

JOACHIM PIANKA

Co-owner of Fein und Ripp

Shot in Berlin

'I have been a lover of old styles from the very beginning. As a 17 year old I used to drive around the countryside, buying and selling old leather jackets from the villages around my birthplace. Whenever I travel I always visit flea markets and old stores.

'The Chopper Pants I'm wearing are from Pike Brothers, and they have the beauty of age. I've worn them for two years now and I love how you can see the variations in the indigo that have been made by wear. The Newsboy Cap, which is also from Pike Brothers, has a minimalistic style and a perfect fit.

'The vest, jacket and shirt are all really special to me: all three are part of our very own collection, which is woven in Hamburg. To be able to produce exactly what we long for in garments is a gift that we are grateful for every day.

'The shoes are from Frye. They are special-edition Prison Boots, and they fit well with the whole idea of the outfit. The pocket watch is a deadstock piece from Doxa. Just like the ones that my two sons have, it is still working flawlessly.'

MARLON PUTZKE

Co-owner of Fein Und Ripp

Shot in Berlin

'My jacket and jeans are both made from an 11-oz denim that is now so smooth/worn-out that you can't really tell that it was ever rigid – it feels more like a suit than rough worker pants.

'Some people might think that the denim-on-denim combination is a bit uniform, but that is exactly what I like about it. My shirt is from our own Fein und Ripp collection. It is simply is an altered NOS (new old stock) army shirt from Sweden. The Frye boots are called Arkansas, and they're in my favourite colour – cognac – which matches the shirt perfectly.'

SIMON GIULIANI

Marketing manager of Candiani Denim

Shot in Milan

'There are three things that I love after my family: denim, travelling and "Made in Italy". In fact, I have collected most of the items in my wardrobe on my trips. I can't resist shopping in good vintage stores, but I love it when new brands try to bring a certain evolution into denimwear. These Purple De Nimes are a great example. They are 100 per cent made in Italy, and their beauty resides entirely in the fabric: a 13-oz tight-construction denim with a grey weft and a beautiful 100 per cent indigo dye. I love wearing them when travelling because they have a slight comfort stretch. Everything else I'm wearing is vintage apart from the jacket and glasses, which are RRL and Ralph Lauren – great brands that help me combine classic elegance with denim tradition.'

ALBERTO CANDIANI

Global manager of Candiani Denim

Shot in Milan

'I was born in a denim mill, so I had no choice. Blue is my blood, but workwear blue, not noble blue. I represent the fourth generation of my family-owned business, and denim is what we do at Candiani, since 1938.

'It took me a second to realize denim was going to be my life – that second happened in the sampling room, where we keep all the jeans we make to show the fabrics in their appropriated "garment form". I started to make all the men's samples in my own size, especially the selvedge line.

'This is what I wear every single day of my life, apart from the occasional wedding or funeral. Here I am wearing a tight-construction 13-oz selvedge denim jean that I have been wearing for over three years and have washed a few times only.'

PIERO TURK

Denim designer

Shot in Milan

'When I was a teenager I really loved the outfits of Chinese people during the Mao period: simple, clean and smart. I also loved the outfits of European workers: blue, strong, simple, with a strong sense of dignity. I think it's probably the smartest look you can find around. And these workers, in Europe, Asia or the US, wearing denims or solid blue garments, were the men who built up our countries, our rights and our democracies – working and fighting hard for their lives but for our freedom as well.

'So my outfit is a tribute to these men and women, a tribute to simple things. A tribute to blue, the colour of workers.'

ANTONIO DI BATTISTA

Consultant and owner of Blue Blanket

Based in Pescara, shot in Milan, Italy

'In this picture I'm wearing a pair of Blue Blanket jeans style P01. This style is the reason I founded my brand. In 2011, after 25 years in the denim business, I decided to produce a five-pocket jean for my friends and myself. It was so successful that everybody pushed me to make a brand.

'Today the collection is composed of 12 styles, all of them are carry-over with the exception of one new style almost every season. The purpose of the brand is to offer to the market a standard product that doesn't reflect trends or fashion; it's like a service for people who want the best ingredients that a pair of jeans can have: 100 per cent pure indigo Japanese selvedge, American classic styling and produced in Italy, plus fit and attention to detail from my long experience working for European brands.

'As you can see, the jeans I'm wearing are not that faded, in fact they were photographed in the first days of their life. Since the start of Blue Blanket I have always worn my jeans for one year until they fall apart. I know that sounds strange, but if you wear a raw jean for 365 days straight and never wash them, you cannot wear them any more! When I stop wearing the jeans, I add them to my archive and use them as inspiration for scraping and fading details.'

DANIEL VERGÉS

Creative director & co-owner at Slowartworks

Shot in Barcelona

'Since I was a child there has always been a lot of music in my house. My parents and brothers have always been music lovers. And even though we like different styles, American roots music was always there: rockabilly, blues, country … That brought me to this style and to a certain way of doing things. I'm a graphic designer and my work is also very influenced by it, the way I approach work from a very organic point of view, giving the maximum importance to the process. I'd say this way of thinking brought me to the world of denim. I'm in love with my Companion jeans, made here in Barcelona by a very talented craftsman, I'm also wearing Edwin, another favourite brand that is finally available here in Barcelona. I also love Levi's Made & Crafted, Red Wing boots and Brixton hats; they have really cool fits.'

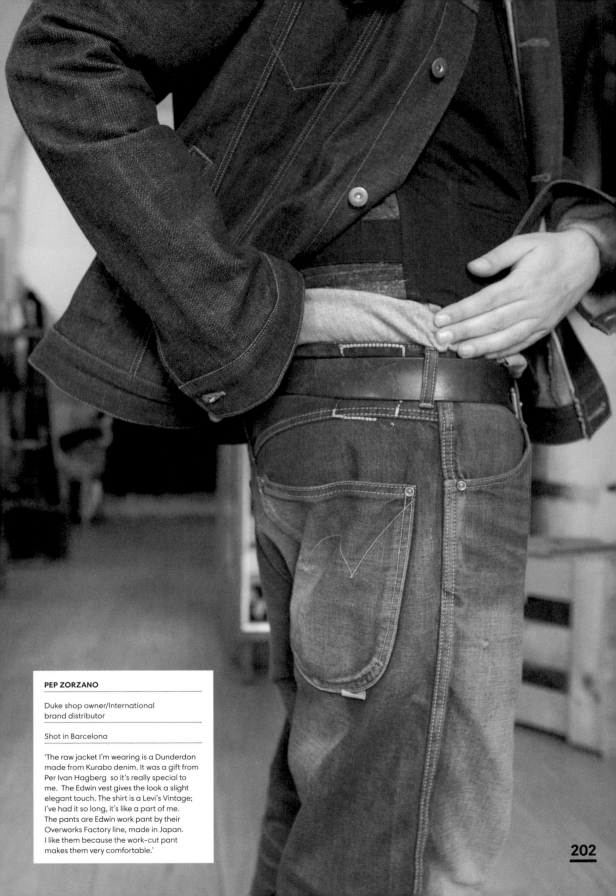

PEP ZORZANO

Duke shop owner/International
brand distributor

Shot in Barcelona

'The raw jacket I'm wearing is a Dunderdon
made from Kurabo denim. It was a gift from
Per Ivan Hagberg so it's really special to
me. The Edwin vest gives the look a slight
elegant touch. The shirt is a Levi's Vintage;
I've had it so long, it's like a part of me.
The pants are Edwin work pant by their
Overworks Factory line, made in Japan.
I like them because the work-cut pant
makes them very comfortable.'

Japan and Australia

Japan has long been known as the epicentre of the authentic and artisan denim scene. Its obsession with American sportswear and the blue jean began during World War II and hit fever pitch in the 1990s with its pursuit of authentic denim: natural indigo, narrow-loom selvedge and vintage machinery replicating the golden era of workwear. More recent brands such as Full Count, Warehouse and Kapital were little known outside of Japan ten years ago, but now these heroes of denim are globally recognised and widely worshipped. Japan's gods of denim reside in Osaka, Kojima, Okayama and Tokyo, as well as in obscure townships and foothills around the country.

Australia is a relative newcomer to the denim scene and houses the misfits of the denim world. These enthusiastic and brave new denim maniacs were led by brands such as Ksubi in the noughties and now stylish and contemporary labels are emerging in their droves. Melbourne is the main breeding ground for fledgling brands such as Neuw, Nobody and Rolla's. Despite this scene's hip and youthful aesthetic, these guys are true denim purists whose main pin-up is a pair of time-worn worker pants.

SHOGO KOIKE

Editor of *2nd Magazine*

Shot in Tokyo

'I found these overalls when I had a job interview for *Lightning Magazine* five years ago. They were deadstock and I fell in love with them. I only wear them on special occasions. I like them because they are so simple; the details are quite basic because they were made during World War II.

'I just love American culture. I used to think every single thing from the States looked so cool, and I think many people of my generation feel the same way. In my opinion, jeans are absolutely the best thing that the Americans ever invented – maybe even the best thing that humans have ever created! It's amazing to think that the five-pocket jean was created 70 years ago, and it's still a perfect shape for everyone today.'

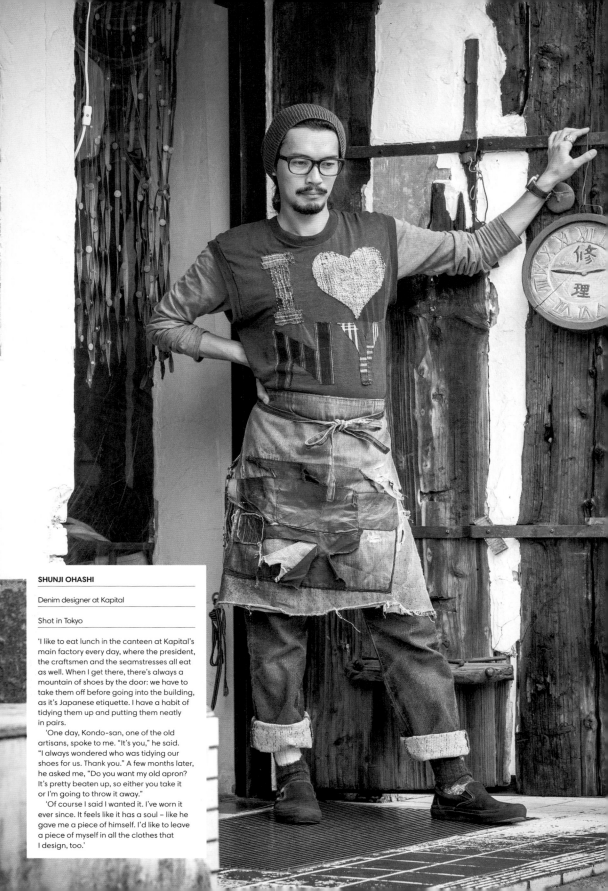

SHUNJI OHASHI

Denim designer at Kapital

Shot in Tokyo

'I like to eat lunch in the canteen at Kapital's main factory every day, where the president, the craftsmen and the seamstresses all eat as well. When I get there, there's always a mountain of shoes by the door: we have to take them off before going into the building, as it's Japanese etiquette. I have a habit of tidying them up and putting them neatly in pairs.

'One day, Kondo-san, one of the old artisans, spoke to me. "It's you," he said. "I always wondered who was tidying our shoes for us. Thank you." A few months later, he asked me, "Do you want my old apron? It's pretty beaten up, so either you take it or I'm going to throw it away."

'Of course I said I wanted it. I've worn it ever since. It feels like it has a soul – like he gave me a piece of himself. I'd like to leave a piece of myself in all the clothes that I design, too.'

RYUICHI ADACHI

Big John designer

Shot in Tokyo

'I break in a lot of raw denim myself. It helps me to understand the fabric better. Each fabric has very different characteristics and the best way to understand that is by wearing the jean. I'm fascinated by the progress and how denim is so different when it's raw and when it's worn-in.

The jean I am wearing here is a pair by Big John in a fabric called "RURI", which is one of Big John's original selvedge denims. Ruri is the Japanese name for lapis lazuli, the deep blue semi-precious stone. Since ancient times, Japanese has used ruri to a describe deep blue/light indigo colour with a hint of purple.

'The denim jacket is also Big John's original selvedge denim called FAUX-SLUB, and it's a new item I am just starting to break in. So I thought I would show both ends of spectrum of denim in my denim-on-denim outfit today!'

RIKIYA KANAMARU

Wrangler lover and owner of Gold Gate

Shot in Matsubara, Tokyo

'In Tokyo, there was a very popular fashion called "shibukaji" in the early 1990s. Shibukaji meant "American casual + work style". The way we interpreted this was by combining jeans with work-style fashion and culture. Looking back now, though, I think we pretty much just misunderstood it!

'It was more like what we saw on American advertisements or posters or in films, and we

Japanese guy who loves denim and the history of American fashion.

'The reason I love Wrangler more than Levi's is because Wrangler produce a more urban design. Since their beginnings, they have always created more than just a design that is useful.

'I have ordered denim specially from Wrangler, and had them change the shape slightly to fit me easily. At the same time, though, I love how they have reintroduced all the details from their original design, such as the oversized denim pants, the imperfect embroidery and patchwork stitching – even the brand stamp on the leather tag. These details are really unique, and they are what set Wrangler apart from other denim brands.'

HITOSHI UCHIDA

Owner of J'Antiques

Shot in Tokyo

'When I first got these jeans, everybody would look at them and say, "Oh that's an amazing vintage Levi replica jean". But in fact they aren't – they are a 501 XX double-side Red Tag from 1954–55. The condition simply seemed too good to be true. However, some of my close friends also have a passion for fine jeans, and they could tell that they were not a replica – because of particular details in the colour, texture and so on.

'At one point, they had a strong musty smell to them, so I washed them many times in hot water in my bathtub to try to get rid of it. A year and a half later, I was washing them again and suddenly realized that they had kept their original colour all this time, which I think is quite special. The only worn parts are some scratches inside the knees from riding my motorcycle.

'I love denim and compare it to growing trees: you can never know what a tree will look like in the future. Denim has its own character and beauty, which continues to grow the longer you wear it.'

ATSUSHI MATSUSHIMA

Editor of *Lightning Magazine*

Shot in Tokyo

'I love to machine-wash my jeans lots of times so that the denim becomes softer and more comfortable, and feels like it's made just for me. My pockets lose colour fast because I always stuff them full of things. The back-right pocket has been fixed once; I was lucky enough to find a guy who could make a flawless repair, and now it looks perfect. I love the colour indigo. The custom-made boots I'm wearing are also very dark navy.

'When I was four, I was burnt by a pot of my grandmother's cooking. The doctor explained that the denim I was wearing was so thick that it saved my skin from more severe burns, which could even have taken my life. So the point of the story is ... denim saved my life!'

HIROSHI TONSHO

Owner of TIME SHOCK (Tokyo) and
TIME 2 SHOCK (Chiba), Japan

Shot in Tokyo

'Pretty much all of my vintage pieces I got
in the 1990s when I lived in Berkeley, San
Francisco. I've been wearing this shirt for
over 20 years now, even though it's falling
apart, because I still love it. I used to buy
all my vintage clothes from the West Coast,
from places like LA or Portland. Later I sold
them in Tokyo; I started a store called TIME
SHOCK in Tokyo, and later opened TIME
2 SHOCK in Kashiwa, Chiba.

'I love this jean jacket. I know it looks like
I've worn it too much already, but it was
basically like this when I found it. That's one
of the reasons I love it. I believe this one is
from the 1940s, known as the WWII model.
There's no cover for the front pocket, and
there are two needles on the back buckle.
I found these 1940s Can't Bust 'Em work
jeans in the States too. They are double
stitched on the side, instead of triple
stitched. The Boro 'Kiriko' scarf was crafted
in Portland, Oregon, but the materials are
from Kiryu, in Japan's Gunma Prefecture, so
for me it's quite special.'

MIKIHARU TSUJITA

Founder of Full Count, Osaka

Shot in Tokyo

'I got these jeans from a friend about three years ago. I could always find cheaper vintage denim, but if the size is too big, nobody brings it back to Japan, so you can't find anything like these here. I always ask my buyer friends to remember me if they spot a larger size!

'About 30 years ago they were still selling Levi's 501 XX in the shops for around 9800 yen (about $100). They were totally different to the new ones, and I loved them. I knew the vintage ones would become more expensive, which they did – more than I expected!

'I love light denim. People think the 501 XX is heavy and uncomfortable because the shape looks tough, but these are only about 13 oz, so they're quite light and comfortable. However, their lightness and age also make them a bit sensitive; the knees tear easily. I used to dislike any rips or tears in my jeans. But now I think these represent good memories, and sometimes a great story you can share. That's the special thing about denim.'

KENICHI SHIOTANI

Co-founder of Warehouse Denim, Tokyo

Shot in Tokyo

'The jeans are Warehouse LOT1008 in a 1940s style. We created this left-hand twill after analyzing data we gathered from a decomposing Levis XX 15 years ago. The Tate-Ochi (worn vertical lines) are longer than the right-hand twill, which is what makes this cowboy-style denim so unique.

'The Chambray shirt is HELLER'S CAFE in a 1930s style and uses indigo rope-dyeing on the warp threads. It has a nice worn look because the threads are still white in the centre. It's hard to see in photos, but we did eyelet work on this shirt, using a very old sewing machine, which gives it a unique and original shape.'

KOUJI SHIOTANI

Co-founder of Warehouse Denim, Tokyo

Shot in Tokyo

'The jeans are Warehouse LOT700 in a 1940s style. This is our newer version of LOT1008 but this denim only uses raw cotton made in Memphis, Tennessee. The right-hand twill that we created is heavier, with more texture, and rough to the touch. The ratio of reduction is quite high, so after you wash the denim it will fit and form to your body in a way which, we have to admit, we simply love. The jacket is HELLER'S CAFE in a 1920s style. This lightweight denim jacket is made using indigo rope-dyeing for the warp threads, and a mock-twist yarn for the weft threads. We just love its simple box-style design.'

JIM THOMPSON

Designer/founder of Three Over One

Shot in Sydney

'Designing my own label gives me the opportunity to take denim fabrics and develop them into anything I wish. My style is like a tailored look from the 1920s and '30s; rather than using wool I like to use denim.

'Here I am wearing a three-piece suit in a heavy indigo Japanese twill with an indigo jacquard camo club collar shirt.

'What underpins everything I do with the label is fabric. I love fabrics that are hardwearing, practical and get better with age. No other fabric does this better than indigo denim. Denim develops its own character and is unique to the wearer. You can tell a lot about a person just by seeing their favourite jeans – in the same way that you can from the wrinkles on their face.'

ANDY PALTOS

Head menswear designer for Threebyone and
co-founder of Rolla's, Melbourne

Shot in Collingwood, Melbourne

'Denim and cars have played a huge part
in my life. In my late teens 1960s classic
cars became an obsession, which led
to vintage denim. I loved the look of the
vintage denim I found, but the fit was never
quite right, which was what got me started
on customization. I started adding darts,
patching, running the legs in, bleaching,
painting them with house paint, etc., which
eventually led me to spending the last ten
years or so designing for denim brands.

'In this photo I am wearing some vintage
jeans I customized back when I first started
getting into denim. The jacket is from
the 1950s. I bought it about ten years
ago from a girl in Kansas whose father
had just passed. He literally spent his life
working in denim: I ended up buying his
whole wardrobe! The vest I bought from
an old biker in Pasadena who used to be
part of the original road crew for Black
Sabbath through the 1970s and '80s, so
it's a special piece.'

TROY STREBE

Denim and wash designer/technician

Shot in Melbourne

'I grew up in the Arizona desert, with parents who were obsessive antique/thrift store/garage sale shoppers. Needless to say, by the age of 17 I had a booming vintage clothing buy/sell business, known as Venus Vintage, selling vintage denim, workwear and historical pieces. Now I design denim with all these aspects in mind.

'I love garments with character and a story. Here I am wearing a 1950s Pay Day 8-oz chore jacket I picked up at a Louisiana garage sale. I love the simplistic shape and its purely utilitarian purpose. It smells like it hasn't been washed since the '50s, and to me that smell is very intriguing – the smell of time.

'Under it is a 1930s Australian goat skin guide's coat. I got it from a friend who rummages through rubbish dumps. This thing is incredible – the number of hand repairs and keyholes, not to mention the incredible aged leather smell. I had to have it. The 1940s Uncle Sam chambray shirt has lived much longer than I expected. I love it for all of the hand-sewn repairs. I can just imagine the scenario: sitting on a rocking chair and mending as years go by.

'The jeans are the only modern thing I'm wearing. They are from Nobody Denim, in 13.5-oz Japanese selvedge denim. I made these puppies myself from cut to bar tack, and I haven't washed them for over a year, apart from bathing in the ocean.'

JASON PAPAROULAS

Creative director of Up There

Shot in Melbourne

'Denim, classic workwear, and all the shades and hues of indigo; there's something that draws me to it all. That sense of character that can be given to each piece over the days, months and years of wear and work that goes into them – it's very distinct to its wearer, almost like a fingerprint.

That's what appeals to me: every shade and crease is a memory forever embossed into the weave and weft of that very pair.

'This pair of NOIRs have been with me for over two years. They're a classic Lee-styled cut, 17-oz Japanese selvedge denim with extremely finite detailing down to the very last stitch of that golden thread. They're built to last, and tell a very specific story. Each paint splash, bleach stain, whisker, honeycomb, stack, rip and scuff defines a moment in their 24 months of wear, and they'll continue to until the jeans fall apart.'

GAV MARTINO

State retail manager of Service Denim Store

Shot in Melbourne

I'm wearing a Neuw Denim Eddie Rebel Jacket in Rebel Wash; the fabric is a stone-washed 13.5-oz right-hand Japanese indigo denim. The jeans are also from Neuw – the Hell Skinny Jean in midnight, profile. The fabric is a 12.5-oz right-hand Italian indigo denim with a black overdye and hand-scraped details.

'I've worked in retail management and product training for over ten years, for and with many denim brands, such as G-Star, Nudie and Acne. During this time I was searching for a brand that valued passion, premium product and denim culture over anything else. Neuw encompasses those values, so I've cemented myself as part of the

PÄR LUNDQVIST

Co-founder/creative director of Neuw

Shot in Melbourne

'I've had these jeans since 2003. They are a pair of Lee 101 B from the 1950s. When I got them I really liked all the details, the fabric and the natural patina. However, the fit was not what I wanted: a very curved, cowboy-style leg and rounded hips. Luckily, I was working with a pattern maker and with his input and expertise, I opened them up, drafted a new pattern on top of the panels, then stitched them back together.

'The result was a pair of jeans that not only represented tradition and craftsmanship but also a sense of currency through a modern slim silhouette. After I re-cut this pair, I started doing it to more and more of the jeans in my archive. All of a sudden I wanted to wear them all. So did my friends.

'I thought to myself, if I ever get the opportunity to start my own brand, this is what I want it to be about. A few years later, I started Neuw with two friends and the design philosophy behind the brand became "vintage revision". So, out of the 3,500 pieces in my vintage collection, I have to say, this is the most important pair. They changed my life.'

PETER LE CHIC

Director of NOIR

Shot in Melbourne

'Being a stickler for detail, I am always curious not just about the outside, but also the inside and construction of a garment. My next question about a garment is "How well would this wear?" When it comes to denim, a couple of months of wear will just not do. I need to feel like we'll be together for years and years. I get attached!

'I'm wearing a NOIR 9-oz shirt with a selvedge placket, a raw 9-oz shirt with a heavy slub and 18-oz NOIR jeans. All three have been well washed. Some pieces I keep raw and never wash; others I'll soak after every five or so wears.'

MISHA HOLLENBACH

Co-founder Perks & Mini

Shot in Melbourne

'To be honest, I rarely wear denim, actually I try to wear as little of anything as possible. Furs and rags are preferred. And that's where boro comes in handy. [Boro means indigo Japanese rags or scraps.] Boro was born of the forgotten values of "mottainai" or "too good to waste", an idea often lacking in the modern consumer lifestyle, and suitable for a lifestyle free of (sometimes) restrictive, uptight fashion. This piece was found in a tiny market stall in Nara. The skull we made for a Stussy UK T-shirt graphic in the mid-2000s. It was nice to dig in our own archive boxes – akin to digging for boro in rural Japan – and to find the old skull. Archaeology and old denim!'

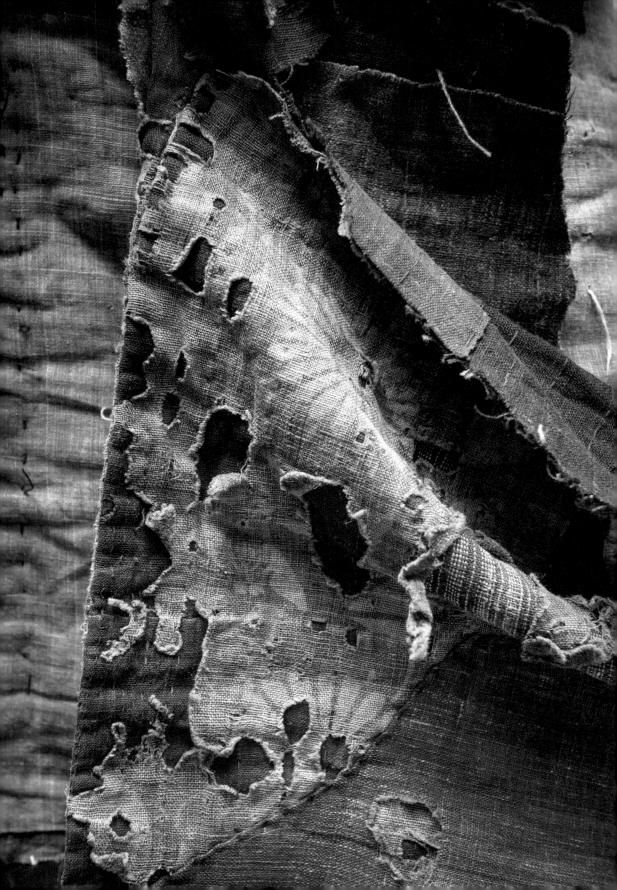

Photographers

SAM CHRISTMAS

FRANCE

Shot: Rey Gautier

Sam Christmas is a London-based portrait photographer who has most recently focused on his passion for motorcycles and has quickly become identified with the custom motorcycle scene in the UK. Last year his personal work on the subject culminated in a solo exhibition called 'Natural Habitats'. Recent clients include Triumph, BMW and leading denim brand, Edwin.

ALBERT COMPER

MELBOURNE & SYDNEY

Shot: Jim Thompson, Andy Paltos, Troy Strebe, Jason Paparoulas, Sav Martino, Pär Lundqvist, Peter Le Chic, Misha Hollenbach

Albert is an eye candy junkie with a penchant for the graphically improbable. He is the brains and the brawn behind the Breakfast Out iPhone app & Sexy Young Things portraiture series. He is a perpetual motion machine whose publications, photographs and schemes will change the world. Yet somehow amidst his passionate professional fervor his respite is the happiness of his wife Laura, daughter Evelyn and their two weird dogs Abelard and Heloise.

TONI MIRET GUAL

BARCELONA

Shot: Daniel Vergés, Pep Zorzano

Born in Barcelona in 1962, Toni studied at Elisava School of Design in Barcelona, before working as a freelance designer and photographer. In 1989 he inaugurated his first studio and since then has combined design and photography. Nowadays the studio is more focused on art directing advertising campaigns – from traditional graphic supports, to video and online communication. Its clients include San Miguel beer, Puma, Nestlé Waters, Carlsberg, Kronenbourg, Mahou, Mariscal Studio and Antonio Miró.

ADAM KATZ SINDING

NEW YORK

Shot: Donwan Harrell, Greg Chapman, Loren Cronk, Herbert Johnson, Ouigi Theodore, Olu Alege, Russell Manley

Raised in the Pacific Northwest, Adam is based in Brooklyn, NY. and now travels the world 90 per cent of the year, following fashion weeks and other interesting social events. He is best known for his website Le 21ème (le-21eme.com) but his work can also be seen in most of the world's top fashion and lifestyle publications.

MAGNUS PETTERSSON

BERLIN

Shot: Daniel Werner, Aljoscha Augustin, Joachim Pianka, Marlon Putzke

Magnus is an interior/portrait photographer working with numerous publications around the world and with interior clients such as Fendi, Warendorf and Fantastic Frank. Born in Chile, Magnus grew up in northern Sweden. After finishing Hedbergska School of Media, he moved to Stockholm and started working as an assistant to photographers such as Martin Adolfsson, Carl Johan Paulin and Vincent Skoglund. He has been based in Berlin since 2009, where, together with friends, he started Studio Fabriken.

TAKUYA SHIMA

TOKYO

Shot: Shogo Koike, Shunji Ohashi, Ryuichi Adachi, Rikiya Kanamaru, Hitoshi Uchida, Atsushi Matsushima, Hiroshi Tonsho, Mikiharu Tsujita, Kenichi Shiotani, Kouji Shiotani

Based in Tokyo, Shima works in New York, LA, Chicago, Hong Kong and throughout Japan. He is a nominee of the International Photography Masters Cup award, and his intriguing photos range from editorial, portrait, commercial and landscape to architectural, and travel, with a primary focus in fashion photography. Exhibitions showcasing his work are on the horizon.

MOLLY CRANNA

LOS ANGELES

Shot: Ken Ito, Kyle J. Pak, Brian Kim, Travis Caine, Mike Hodis, Maurizio Donadi, Benjamin Phillips, Rob Harmsen

A graduate of the USC School of Cinematic Arts and based in LA, Molly specializes in editorial portraits and bold still-lifes. Her work can be seen in major publications such as *Glamour*, *Bon Appetit*, *Elle China*, and *Travel+Leisure*.

KELLY FOBER

AMSTERDAM

Shot: René Strolenberg, Jason Denham, Pierre Morissette, Menno Van Meurs, Olaf Hussein, Tony Tonnaer

Kelly was born in Eindhoven, and is currently living in Rotterdam. A young photographer experimenting with different directions of photography at the Willem de Kooning Academy, she loves to combine different genres such as fashion, portrait, street and architecture. Her creative vision comes to the fore when she works on concepts for new works.

VALENTINA FRUGIUELE

PARIS

Shot: Brice Partouche, Katsu Manabe, François Girbaud, Philip Rudjeanski, Miles Johnson

Valentina is an Italian photographer based in Paris. Her main focus has always been portraying people, through fashion and portrait photography. She did lots of editorial for international magazines and after a few years discovered that street style photography allowed her to combine fashion with the more natural and spontaneous side of people. Her work is now focused on portrait photography, taking pictures of famous or soon-to-be-famous actors and personalities.

RYAN LOPEZ

LOS ANGELES

Shot: Olivier Grasset, Christophe Loiron, Larry McKaughan, Adriano Goldshmied, Zip Stevenson

Born on a farm and raised by wolves, Ryan is first and foremost an adventurer and a lover of new experience. He receives inspiration from the people he comes into contact with and the places he has the privilege to visit. His mode of expression comes through photography. Classically trained in art, advertising and photography, he translates every moment of his life into a visual exploration. Ryan is currently based in Los Angeles, California but is constantly travelling for work.

ULYSSES ORTEGA

SAN FRANCISCO

Shot: Jonathan Lukacek, Nick Kemp, John Alburl, Kiya Babzani, Bart Sights

Ulysses Ortega is a photographer based out of San Francisco, CA. Shooting primarily with 35mm film, his work focuses on rhythm, form, and space. Ortega has travelled to Japan, Mexico, and Sweden with photography to document a number of endeavours, all unified by an interest in origins and culture. He has produced work for international clients including *Plus 81 Magazine*, Nudie Jeans, and Steven Alan.

NICOLÒ PARSENZIANI

MILAN

Shot: Simon Giuliani, Antonio Di Battista, Alberto Candiani, Piero Turk

Nicolò lives and works as a freelance photographer in Milan while studying Architecture at the Polytechnic of Milan. He has worked for numerous magazines and brands including Vogue.it, Style.it, Blumarine and Emilio Pucci.

STEPHANIE SIAN-SMITH

LONDON

Shot: Dave Carroll, Shaka Maidoh, Sam Lambert, Doug Gunn, Mark Westmoreland, Mark Wilsmore, Rudy Rupen Budhdeo, Henry Holland, Huggy Leaver, Mohsin Sajid, Fergadelic

A graduate of Design at Bristol UWE and Photography at LCC, Stephanie is based in East London. She has worked for *Clash, Elle, I- D magazine, Another* online, *Dazed & Confused, Vice, Grazia* and *Art Review*. She had her debut solo show 'I've Done Alright For A Girl' in April 2012 and her latest exhibition 'Pusszine' (Sept 2014) is a celebration of girls and cats.

MÄRTA THISNER

STOCKHOLM & GOTHENBURG

Shot: Örjan Andersson, Hakim Krim, Axel Nyhage, Klas Erixon, Carl Malmgren, Johan Lindstedt, Elias Jubran

Märta Thisner is a photographer living in Stockholm. She loves her work, most of which is for magazines and books, covering the worlds of music, fashion and art.

Amy Leverton

Amy has been working in the denim industry since 2003; for four years as a denim and casual wear designer and then in trend forecasting and consultancy.

Her career started at the niche collaborative company Oki-ni, in London, where she worked with denim brands such as Lee and Evisu. During this time she worked on a limited White Oak selvedge jean for Duffer St. George and visited the legendary Cone Mills plant in Greensboro, North Carolina. She took Cone's three-day course in denim, which became the defining moment that led to her passion for indigo.

In 2007 she entered the world of trend analysis, working for the UK's leading online trend forecasting website, WGSN before heading over to US competitor Stylesight in 2010, where she is currently head of Denim and Youth Culture at the newly relaunched WGSN product.

Amy's day job encompasses reporting and analysis of the denim market; she covers over 20 industry trade shows annually, analysing street style, scouring fashion week runway shows and hunting for obscure new brands as well as attending one-off events, vintage shows and music festivals around the globe. An average year means visiting Los Angeles, New York, Paris, Las Vegas, Amsterdam, San Francisco and Berlin in search of denim innovation.

Acknowledgements

Thank you Dude!

Sam Trotman, Ralph Tharpe, Lu Franquesa, Marek Steven, Frank Bober, Vito Plantamura, Remco De Nijs, Nicolai Sclater, Ricardo Hernandez, Scott Anderson, Guilio Miglietta, Neil Leverton, Robert G. Leach, Neil Elliott, Greg Hewitt, Peter Jones, Mohsin Sajid.

And of course all the dudes, with special thanks to: Mark Westmoreland, Zip Stevenson, Rudy Rupen Budhdeo, Greg Chapman, Piero Turk, Kiya Babzani, Atsushi Matsushima, Andy Paltos, Tony Tonnaer.

And all the photographers, with special thanks to:
Albert Comper and Takuya Shima

Thank you Dudette!

Helen Job, Shannon Davenport, Laura Weir, Amanda Gilbert, Jenny Shima, Sue Barrett, Kara Nicholas, Claire Foster, Amber Prettyman, Helen Sac, Liza Mackenzie, Shanu Walpita, Kelly Miller, Kathleen Tso, Marianne Leverton, Susie Draffan, Kelly Dawson, Carri Munden, Helen Rochester, Sanna Charles.

All the photographers, with special thanks to:
Stephanie Sian-Smith and Märta Thisner.

Published in 2015 by
Laurence King Publishing Ltd
361–373 City Road
London EC1V 1LR

e-mail: enquiries@laurenceking.com
www.laurenceking.com

Reprinted 2015

A catalogue record for this book is available from the British Library.

ISBN: 978-1-78067-418-6

Design: Design by St
Senior Editor: Peter Jones
Printed in China